WHALES
and DOLPHINS
of Newfoundland & Labrador

WAYNE LEDWELL

Copyright Wayne Ledwell, 2005

Library and Archives Canada Cataloguing in Publication

Ledwell, Wayne, 1954-
Whales and Dolphins of Newfoundland and Labrador / Wayne Ledwell.

ISBN 0-9730271-5-0

1. Whales—Newfoundland and Labrador. 2. Dolphins—Newfoundland
and Labrador. I. Title.

QL737.C4L42 2005   599.5'09718
C2005-902574-3

9 8 7 6 5 4 3 2 1

Boulder Publications Ltd.
Published and printed in Canada

Digital whale illustrations by Elaine Frampton
Layout & design by John Andrews

Front cover humpback & back cover humpback tail photographs by Deb Young,
courtesy of O'Brien's Whale and Bird Tours. Back cover common dolphin photo-
graph by Patrick Abgrall & humpback by Claudio Corbelli.

Assistance provided by the Government of Newfoundland and Labrador

CONTENTS

Claudio Corbelli, Whale Research Group
Humpback whale lobtailing on its back in Witless Bay.

Newfoundland and Labrador offers some of the best opportunities for viewing whales and dolphins anywhere in the world.

This guide provides information needed to identify these animals. It is also useful in identifying those that become stranded on shore.

Guide books themselves are intended only as an aid, however. Nothing can beat the knowledge and familiarity gained by seeing these animals in the wild. I was once at sea with conservation officers who spend much of their time on the water. These are people who frequently see whales, but no one had shown them what to look for when distinguishing different species. But after spotting whales with them for only a short time, they had become as adept as I am.

I hope you will find this book informative and useful.

Jason Yetman, watching white-beaked dolphins off Triangle, Labrador at the opening to White Bear Arm. (Hollis Yetman)

INTRODUCTION

IDENTIFICATION TIPS

We often get only fleeting glances of whales. But pay attention: Identification is usually based upon the height and shape of the blows, and whether or not a dorsal fin is present.

Watch the water and listen carefully to the whale's blow. This "puff of smoke" can be important when trying to identify whales. Note the shape, size and direction of the blow. The number of blows and time spent submerged between blows depends on whether the animal is feeding, searching for food, or moving on. The identification of a blow is not an exact science, however, because of distortions by wind and sea conditions.

The blow is often followed by a quick view of the animal. Can you determine how long the body is? Does it have a dorsal fin? How big is the fin and where is it on the whale's body?

The tail can also be used to identify a whale species. Does the whale lift its tail above the water surface, and if so, at what angle? How high is the tail lifted above the water? What is the size, shape and colour of the tail?

Tail colouration and scarring can be important clues to identifying individual animals. In particular, such markings have made it possible to track the lives and migration patterns of the humpback whale. About 5,000 northwest Atlantic humpback whale tails have been catalogued for individual identification. Other whales, such as the blue, are identified and catalogued by variations in skin pigmentation, which occur as circle patterns and shades of colour.

Some whales may also lift their heads to the water surface, a behaviour known as spy-hopping. This, too, helps identify species. More often, however, we see only an animal's blow, back and tail.

All of this information needs to be gathered in just a few moments, before the animal dives. This glimpse is all a person with experience usually needs to make an accurate identification. This knowledge has been used since man began hunting whales for food, oil and other commercial purposes.

But even people used to seeing whales can experience difficulty identifying some species. Juvenile fin, sei and minke whales look similar, for example, even up close. Dolphins can also be difficult to identify, because they often display similar colour patterns and are similar in size.

WHALE WATCHING

In Newfoundland and Labrador we are lucky to have the largest population of humpbacks in the northwest Atlantic. Humpbacks are also one of the easiest whales to identify. For these reasons, this species is the main focus of whale watching in Newfoundland. You may recognize them by their "bushy"- shaped blow and by their long white side fins – the size of an airplane propeller – that they sometimes slap on the water surface in a behaviour called flippering. They are also very acrobatic and you may observe them leap clear out of the water. This is called breaching. Humpbacks will frequently raise their tail before diving. The colour patterns on their tails are unique to each animal and are used by scientists to identify and track individuals.

Humpbacks have predictable migration patterns. They can be regularly observed in Newfoundland waters during late spring, summer and fall. Early in the season, some prime areas for viewing humpbacks are on the Avalon Peninsula – including St. John's, the Witless Bay Ecological Reserve, Trinity Bay and around Twillingate. In September, humpbacks are more abundant along the Northern Peninsula.

Humpbacks migrate to Newfoundland to feed on schooling fish, such as capelin and herring. Simply ask local fishermen for areas of particular abundance of fish. This is where you will most likely find humpbacks.

There are several options for watching whales along the coasts of Newfoundland and Labrador. They can be seen during a ferry ride from Nova Scotia, and basically from any point along the shores of this province.

An interesting spot to enjoy these animals is from the beach of St. Vincent's on the southern shore of the Avalon Peninsula. Here, humpbacks can be seen feeding close to land – you just have to stand on the beach with your camera at the ready.

If you are interested in a closer encounter, you can take one of the many commercial boat tours offered around the province. These companies operate in all areas of high whale concentrations. There are about fifty operators in the island portion of the province, some of which have been active since the 1980s. Whale tours vary in length, price and type. You can go on a more comfortable tour boat, complete with onboard bar service and live entertainment. Alternately, you can opt for an adventurous ride in a zodiac.

Whatever your choice, before taking part in a trip, you should inquire about which ones operate in the most environmentally responsible way. Look for those that subscribe to the Newfoundland

and Labrador whale-watching voluntary code of conduct. This set of rules has been established in collaboration with scientists at Memorial University to reduce the impact of boat traffic on the animals. The code of conduct also ensures a safe environment for passengers, and stipulates that they receive an educational experience.

Tour-boat operators must respect a 100-metre minimum distance from whales. They must also avoid chasing whales, and are prohibited from cutting-off their path or boxing them in.

It is important to remember that humpback whales are in Newfoundland and Labrador waters for survival purposes, including feeding and socializing. If a whale is disturbed in areas of high concentrations of prey, it may fail to gain necessary energy supplies for migrating to tropical breeding grounds.

STUDYING WHALES

Most species of whales in the waters of Newfoundland and Labrador are seasonal migrants. In spring and summer, they travel to rich feeding grounds in the northern latitudes. Migration to warmer, southern latitudes takes place in late fall and early winter. The large whale species mate and calve in these tropical areas.

Along the coasts of Newfoundland and Labrador the animals find dense concentrations of schooling fish such as capelin, herring, and mackerel. The immense biological productivity of these waters also provides food for a wide variety of other marine animals and seabirds – and for humans. This fact is enunciated by writer Harold Horwood in his description of the island of Belle Isle: "This is a land that belongs to migrant seals and world-girdling whales, to great floating mountains of ice, glacier blue and sea green… and to hidden shoals of fish whose world is always just on the borderline of ice."

Our knowledge of many whale species is sparse. Little is known about many beaked whales, for example, because they live in remote regions of the world's oceans. These areas are expensive to get to and study, and the animals rarely enter shallow near-shore waters. Beaked whales also have long dive times, a trait that makes them difficult to track. Even when observed, positive identification is difficult. There are only slight differences in colour, size, shape of the forehead and length of the beak. In Newfoundland and Labrador, knowledge about Sowerby's beaked whales and pygmy sperm whales has been gained only through strandings. Their deaths offer tantalizing glimpses into the life histories of these secretive animals.

Ironically, those who hunted and killed whales have given us a great deal of knowledge about population numbers, stock structures and migration patterns of the largest whales. Information about the biology of whales came primarily through whale hunting. Much was learned on the decks of whaling ships and on the wharves of shore stations, by scientists working alongside men who killed the animals. With the end of widespread hunting of whales, studies have focused on their ecology, how they associate with one another and what regions they frequent. This new information, combined with historical whale-hunting data, helps us piece together the life histories of these animals.

BALEEN AND TOOTHED WHALES

Whales and dolphins belong to the order Cetacea and are divided into two sub-orders: the mysticeti, or baleen whales, and the odontoceti, or toothed whales. Dolphins are actually toothed whales.

Generally, whales are categorized based on the presence of teeth or baleen. There are twelve baleen whale species. They have baleen plates, which they use in place of teeth for feeding. Baleen whales have two nostrils, while toothed species have just one.

The sixty-seven species of toothed whales differ in the size, number, and placement of teeth. Sperm whales have teeth only in their lower jaws. Dolphins have teeth in both jaws.

Some beaked whales, such as the Sowerby's and bottlenose, have as few as two teeth in their lower jaws. Among these species – and

Claudio Corbelli, Whale Research Group
Humpback whale in Witless Bay with a research tag attached.

Wayne Ledwell

Pilot whale stranded at Lewisporte. It was successfully rescued and released into the wild.

usually only among males – these teeth may be seen protruding out-side the jaw. Then there is the narwhal – the male sports a long tusk, which is actually one of his front teeth. The harbour porpoise has numerous small, chisel-shaped teeth. These whales do not use their teeth for chewing, but rather for catching and grasping prey. Food is swallowed whole.

Baleen whales are named for their specialized arrangement of feeding structures. These large whales range from the smaller seven-metre-long minke to the largest animal that has ever lived on our planet, the thirty-metre-long blue whale.

Baleen, or whalebone as it was known during the era of commer-cial whale hunting, is a hard, flexible substance, similar in composi-tion to hair and fingernails. It is used to sieve food from the water. Baleen whales have a large mouth in which anywhere from 150 to 400 triangular pieces of baleen hang down like a curtain from each side of the upper jaw. Individual baleen pieces range from four-metres in length in the bowhead to less than half-a-metre in the minke. Whales gulp or skim large quantities of water, containing thousands of small schooling fish, shrimp, or plankton. They then close their mouths and use their huge tongues to force the water out through the hairy fringes of the baleen. Food is then trapped in the

Deb Young, courtesy O'Brien's Whale & Bird Tours

Baleen whales have two nostrils, toothed whales one nostril. Above: Humpback whale on the southern shore of the Avalon Peninsula. Below: Northern bottlenose whale in the Davis Strait.

Wayne Ledwell

baleen and swallowed.

In spite of their size differences, all species of whales and dolphins are similar in many ways. Their bodies are streamlined, hairless and smooth – except for whisker-like hairs on the snouts of some species. All have thick layers of insulating blubber under their skin. They have side fins and large, powerful horizontal tail flukes. All but a few also have dorsal fins. In addition, all whales have blowholes on the tops of their heads that are used for breathing.

All baleen whale species in Newfoundland and Labrador waters, with the exception of the bowhead, undertake long migratory journeys from warm equatorial breeding areas to temperate and polar feeding areas.

The author's daughter, Abigail, with a sperm whale jaw and holding a section of baleen.

During their time on the feeding grounds they eat voraciously and constantly, putting on fat reserves they need to sustain them during four to six months of fasting in the lower latitudes.

Unlike baleen species, most toothed whales living in our waters do not travel extensively. Belugas and narwhals move with the ebb and flow of the pack ice, rarely straying far from it. Dolphins travel back and forth into and out of coastal areas along the continental shelf. Male sperm whales undertake the similar north-south migrations of baleen whales, while females usually stay in temperate waters year-round.

STRANDINGS AND ICE-ENTRAPMENTS

Throughout history, stranded whales and dolphins have provided a windfall of food for people living in coastal communities. All species of whales and dolphins living off Newfoundland and Labrador have stranded here. Many strandings are of single animals, but there have been notable instances of mass strandings – in 1979, there was a stranding of 139 pilot whales at Point au Gaul on the Burin Peninsula. Ice-entrapments, particularly of white-beaked dolphins, occur regularly here during winter and spring when shifting pack ice traps them.

The reasons for whale and dolphin strandings, and why many are unable to survive after being pushed or towed back out to sea, are unclear. Some theories include parasitic infections, orientation difficulties, and pods of animals following a sick leader. On the other hand, a group of animals may simply find itself in the wrong place at the wrong time. From a scientific perspective, strandings offer a window into the life histories of some of the world's most elusive species. Mass strandings can present a large sample size for research purposes.

If you see a stranded marine animal, you should not attempt to interfere with it. Instead, call the local office of the federal Department of Fisheries and Oceans.

There is also a hotline number available: 1-888-895-3003.

ENTRAPMENTS IN FISHING GEAR

The incidental entrapment of whales in fishing gear is a serious worldwide threat to the survival of many species. From 1978 to 2004, more than 1,300 humpbacks alone were reported entrapped in fishing gear in Newfoundland and Labrador.

Procedures for safely disentangling whales were designed by Jon Lien of Memorial University, a method in use today, both here and other areas of the world. Releasing entrapped whales is done with the assistance of fish harvesters in this region – a program that has saved money and countless hours of lost time. The program has also saved the lives of hundreds of whales.

HUNTING AND OTHER THREATS

Red Bay, a community on the southern coast of Labrador, was a busy area for whalers in the early 1500s. The Basques, who had been hunting whales since 1000 A.D. throughout the northern seas of Europe, began pursuing northern right and bowhead whales to North America. Red Bay was the site of the first oil-production station in our waters. Today, there is a wonderful museum of Basque whaling history at Red Bay. Among the artifacts on display at this museum are bones from whales slaughtered by the Basques, as well as the tools used by whalers. Remnants of ships upon which they sailed are on display, as well as the graves of whalers who died in Red Bay.

Jon Lien

A group of dead pilot whales, mass stranded at Point au Gaul.

Jon Lien

A dead blue whale stranded on the west coast of Newfoundland.

Wayne Ledwell

Humpback whale snared in a cod trap at Valleyfield, a community formally known as Whale's Gulch.

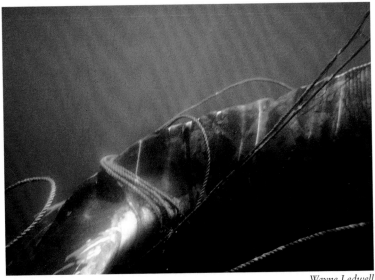

Wayne Ledwell

Cod trap rope is seen wrapped around the torso of a humpback whale, entangled in nets near Petite Forte.

Whales were hunted for their blubber, which was boiled down to produce oil. Baleen was also sought for manufacturing corsets, umbrellas and whips. Prior to the invention of the harpoon gun, whalers concentrated on hunting right and sperm whales. The right whale was favoured because it was comparatively easy to catch – it frequents coastal waters, is a slow swimmer, and contains so much fat that they float when killed. Right whales were also productive – 3,000 gallons of oil could be rendered from one animal. It thus acquired the name right whale simply because it was the right whale to hunt. Together with the sperm whale, right whales constituted the bulk of commercial whale hunting prior to the advent of faster ships and more effective killing techniques.

Large, swift whales, including the blue, fin and sei, had largely escaped traditional hunters because whalers could not catch them. This changed with the invention of the harpoon gun by a Norwegian, Svend Foyn, in the mid-1860s.

The harpoon gun and the introduction of fast, steam-powered whaling ships gave hunters critical advantages when pursuing the larger whale species. These technological advances, combined with demand for whale products by the cosmetics and pet-food industries, provided incentives to hunt the bigger whales.

Whaling took place on a scale never seen before, making possible the killing of 750,000 fin whales in Antarctica alone. In Newfoundland and southern Labrador, almost 20,000 blue, fin, sei, humpbacks and sperm whales, and over 50,000 pilot whales, had been processed at whaling stations by the time commercial whale hunting ended in our waters in 1972.*

The unrestrained hunting of whales around the world led to the creation of the International Whaling Commission (IWC) shortly after World War II. Restrictions on hunting gradually tightened during the ensuing decades as whale populations declined.

In 1982, members of the IWC agreed to end commercial hunting of large whales. Limited hunting of some whale species, such as the minke, has been maintained by a few nations – most notably Norway and Japan – despite the moratorium. In North America, no whaling occurs, with the exception of a few bowheads taken yearly by indigenous peoples in Alaska and the eastern Arctic.

Uncontrolled hunting severely reduced populations of most large whale species. Unfortunately, the path back to recovery is proving complex. Some species, such as the right, bowhead and blue, have not recovered despite a decades-long hunting ban. Only 300 northern right – and maybe a similar number of blue – whales remain in the north Atlantic, and the challenge to save this species is proving

Jack Lawson

A bowhead being butchered near Cross Island, Alaska, in a small scale aboriginal hunt.

A dead northern bottlenose whale, captured by Norwegian whalers, prior to the moratorium on hunting this species.

difficult. Right whales are still being lost, primarily from ship strikes and entanglements in fishing gear. Other species, such as the humpback, appear to be recovering, but many challenges remain.

Most of the world's large whales must travel long distances

between feeding grounds and breeding areas. Humpback migratory patterns are well understood. But the habits of other species, such as the fin and blue, are largely unknown.

Whales have long, complex migratory routes that cover thousands of kilometres and overlap the territorial waters of many countries. In their travels, whales must pass through oceans filled with fishing gear. They must negotiate shipping channels where ships may strike them. They must also deal with recreational vessels and whale-watching boats.

The problems of habitat destruction and pollution pose additional threats to all whale species. Large industrial developments may compromise their habitat. Toxic substances can be passed through the food chain, possibly poisoning and killing whales.

Whales are particularly sensitive to noise. For example, bowhead whalers would often sail up to an animal in order to harpoon it, because the animals could hear them approaching if oars were used. Whales live in an acoustic world and can be adversely affected by noises associated with human activities on the ocean. These hazards include seismic surveys used for oil and gas exploration, military sonar, and even the motors of ships – including whale-watching vessels.

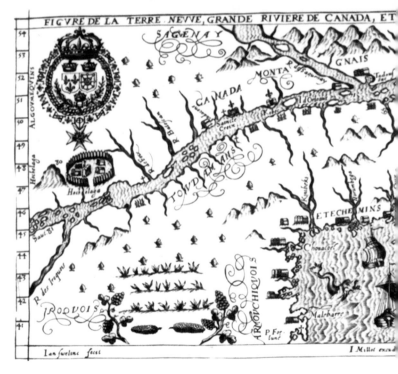

Any harassment affects the basic needs of a whale, because they must feed, mate, calve and care for their young.

Declining fish stocks also pose a serious threat to whales. We are fishing further and further down the food chain, and now harvest such animals as capelin, shrimp and even krill. These organisms are vital to the survival of whales, seabirds and larger fish.

In Canada, the status of whale species is reviewed periodically by scientists, in conjunction with community members. Findings are reported to the Committee on the Status of Endangered Wildlife in Canada. COSEWIC, along with marine-mammal scientists, assesses populations and distribution trends. Recommendations are then made regarding research and whether further actions are necessary for the protection of whale species.

*In 1904, 1,275 whales were landed at fourteen whaling stations operated around the coasts of Newfoundland and Labrador by Norwegian whalers.

Below: A French map from 1609, showing Newfoundland, Labrador and Nova Scotia. Whales are depicted as sea monsters.

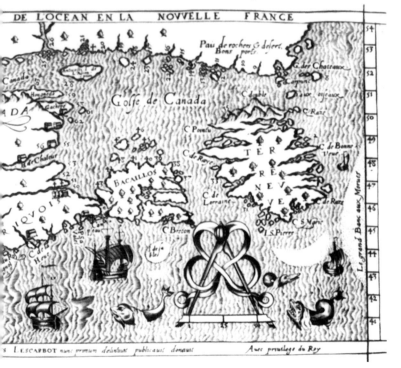

BLUE WHALE
(Balaenoptera musculus)

IDENTIFICATION
- World's largest animal (30 metres)
- Mottled grey and blue
- Tallest blow of any whale
- Small dorsal fin, set well back on body
- Lifts tail at an angle, rather than vertically
- Can be confused with fin whales
- Massive jaws
- Black baleen up to one metre long
- 60 to 88 throat grooves
- Long tapered pectoral fins are greyish underneath
- Broad triangular tail flukes
- Algae growing on belly may give it a creamy colour

DISTRIBUTION

Blue whales are a cosmopolitan species, with a range that extends from the pack ice around each of the poles to temperate and tropical waters. The worldwide population of blue whales is estimated to be less than 12,000. Two populations exist in the northern hemisphere – one off eastern Canada and the other in the western north Pacific. Their known north Atlantic range is east from Iceland to the Gulf of St. Lawrence. Sporadic sightings are reported off the Scotian Shelf to the northern Gulf of Maine. Blue whales are occasionally seen in Conception, Trinity and Placentia bays during the summer months. They are more commonly sighted from May to December and some throughout the winter in the northern Gulf of St. Lawrence regions. It is unclear how far blue whales migrate, and the major wintering and calving grounds are not known. Up to 400 blue whales have been photographed and catalogued in the northwest Atlantic by scientists, mostly in the Gulf of St. Lawrence.

From the 1970s to 1992, thirty-one blue whales were reportedly killed by pack ice along the southwest coast of Newfoundland. The

Jon Lien, Whale Research Group

An aerial view of a blue whale surfacing.

animals, which feed on krill at the ice edges, become trapped as ice breaks up in the spring and pushes the whales into shallow water.

IDENTIFICATION

The blue whale is the world's largest animal, the longest recorded being thirty-three metres. The U-shaped head has a single prominent ridge running down the middle.

The colour is mottled with irregular blue, white and grey spots. The dorsal fin is small (30 cm long) in relation to those of other baleen whales. It is located on the last quarter of the body and is seen as the whale arches its back to dive. The flippers are long, tapered and grey on the underside.

The tail is dark, broad and triangular in shape and has a notch in the middle. The underside of a blue whale's tail is rarely seen, unlike other species such as humpbacks and sperm whales. As a blue whale dives, the tail rises at an angle, rather than vertically, and they often do not even lift their tails above the surface before dives. This whale has a tall, thunderous, straight blow, rising to a height of seven metres.

Due to their size, blue whales can easily be confused with fin whales. However, at closer range, body pigmentation and size and position of the dorsal fin are distinguishing features, as are the size and height of the blow.

Patrice Corbeil

Blue whales have small dorsal fins and are mottled in colour.

BIOLOGY

These whales typically weigh 100 tonnes – as heavy as twenty-five elephants – and are longer than the largest jumbo jet. Blues with a length of thirty-three metres and a weight of about 190 tonnes have been recorded in the Antarctic. One twenty-seven metre-long Antarctic blue whale processed at a whaling station in the 1920s had a tongue the size of an adult elephant, and a heart weighing half a tonne – so large that a seven-year-old child would be able to crawl through its chambers. Cruising the world's oceans, blue whales feed in the productive waters of the continental shelves and ice pack edges. This, the largest animal, feeds on some of the smallest – krill and shrimp – which form into large, dense concentrations. Blue whales need to eat two to four tonnes of this food each day.

The life span of the blue whale is thought to be similar to that of humans. They become sexually mature at five to seven years of age and mate every two years. Pregnancies last one year, and the mother nurses her calf for six months. Newborns are more than seven metres long and weigh in excess of two tonnes. A blue whale grows fast, gaining 100 kilograms every day on its mother's rich, fatty milk. By seven months, a baby blue whale is sixteen metres long and weighs twenty-three tonnes.

Wayne Ledwell

A blue whale off Bellevue, Trinity Bay.

HUMAN INTERACTION

Scientists and whalers gathered information on biology, population structure and areas of occurrence during the whale-hunting era. By 1965, after fifty years of hunting in the Antarctic, more than 200,000 blue whales had been killed. The population was decimated, and it was estimated that fewer than 10,000 animals remained worldwide following the cessation of hunting.

In Newfoundland and Labrador, where a smaller population of the animals lived, hunting pressures drove the blue whale to commercial extinction. From 1898 until 1951, when the commercial hunting of blue whales ended in the western north Atlantic, Newfoundland whaling stations landed 1,446 blues.

Blue whales face many challenges to their survival, and the species remains endangered. With so few individuals remaining, the opportunities for rebuilding their population are hindered by the loss of just a few animals every year to such hazards as ice entrapments and entanglements with fishing gear. With so few of their kind left, any mortality reduces the chances that this species will survive.

FIN WHALE
(Balaenoptera physalus)

IDENTIFICATION
- Second largest whale (20 metres)
- Dark blue-grey back
- Skin is not mottled as with blue whales
- Right side (only) of jaw is yellowish-white
- Does not usually raise tail flukes when diving

- Tall blow, rising up to five metres
- Yellow-white baleen on right side, black baleen on left side
- Baleen plates up to 90 cm long
- 56 to 100 throat grooves
- White belly
- Flippers white underneath

DISTRIBUTION
The fin whale can be found in most areas of the world, with current global populations estimated to be in the tens of thousands. In the north Atlantic, fin whales range from the Gulf of Mexico to the Arctic pack ice.

Fin whales are commonly found in Newfoundland and Labrador waters from early spring to late fall and can be seen throughout the region. They are often seen in the same areas as humpbacks, but tend to stay further offshore in deeper waters. Good viewing areas are off southern Labrador, particularly the Strait of Belle Isle, but they are also seen off southeastern Newfoundland. The waters of Newfoundland and Labrador appear to represent a major feeding area for fin whales in the north Atlantic; however, mating and calving areas have not yet been identified for these animals, and their migration patterns are not well understood.

Fin whale.   Pat Abgrall

IDENTIFICATION

Next to the humpback, the fin whale is the most numerous of the large whale species in Newfoundland and Labrador waters. Whales can usually be identified by the shape and height of their blows, although weather conditions and distances can cause confusion. A large, tall blow will likely be that of either a humpback or a fin whale. The blow of a fin whale is prominent, rising to five metres, while a humpback blow is shorter and bushier in appearance.

Fin whales are sleek, with a dark grey to black back, and eighteen to twenty-three metres in length. Their tall, hooked dorsal fin is set two-thirds of the way down their body. Fin whales do not usually lift their tail flukes when diving.

The animals often surface together in groups, and typically blow five to ten times before submerging. There are times when fin whales will appear oblivious to boat traffic in their area, and individuals have been known to cruise slowly towards and underneath a vessel, while remaining clearly visible in the water. Fin whales are known to breach, but this is rarely observed.

The fin whale is the only mammal with consistently asymmetrical colouration. The right side of the jaw and baleen are yellowish-white, while the left side of the jaw and baleen are dark.

The head of the fin whale is more streamlined than the U-shaped of the head of the blue whale, a species with which it is often confused. Some fin whales have grey bands (called chevrons) behind their heads that sweep down over their sides. Those bands or stripes, together with overall pigmentation patterns, dorsal fin shapes and scars, are used by scientists to identify individual animals. Due to their size, fin whales can be easily confused with the other whales, particularly blue and sei whales.

Danielle Dion

A fin whale, lunge feeding in the Bay of Fundy.

BIOLOGY

After the blue whale, the fin whale is the second-largest animal on the planet. It is also one of the fastest, capable of bursts of speed in excess of thirty kilometres per hour. Named for its high dorsal fin, it also has been given local names, such as finback and finner. Fin whales are one of the greatest long-distance travelers of the natural world, with one animal tagged in Iceland swimming 3,000 km in only ten days. Their speed and sleekness give fin whales the title "greyhounds of the ocean." Fin whales are capable of making extremely loud, low-frequency sounds, which can be detected over hundreds of kilometres in deep water.

In Newfoundland and Labrador, fin whales feed on a variety of small schooling fish, such as capelin and herring, as well as krill.

Fin whales become sexually mature at seven to ten years of age. Pregnancies last for about one year, after which a six-metre-long calf is born, weighing about two tonnes. A calf will nurse for six to eight months, at which point it will be eleven metres long. A female fin whale will usually have a calf every two to three years. They become physically mature at about fifteen years of age and have a life span comparable to humans.

HUMAN INTERACTION

Interactions with fin whales are often memorable because the animals are so huge and sleek. There are times when the animals will let boats approach, and individuals may remain in the same geographic area for several days.

Fin whale lunge feeding.   Danielle Dion

In Newfoundland and Labrador, the fin whale was the basis of the modern whaling industry. Of the total recorded catch for large whales, sixty-six per cent of them were fins, with 12,859 killed. Most of those fin whales were landed at the Aquaforte whaling station on the southern shore of the Avalon Peninsula. Some 3,000 fin whales currently live in the northwest Atlantic. While numbers appear to be increasing in some areas, the species is still considered depleted at a global level.

Fin whale and dolphins.   Jon Lien

SEI WHALE
(Balaenoptera borealis)

IDENTIFICATION
- Large whale (up to 16 metres)
- Dark, bluish-grey in colour
- Tall, slender dorsal fin
- Flippers are small and pointed
- Tail is small in relation to body size
- Blow not as tall as fin or blue whales
- Baleen is very fine and up to 80 cm long
- Baleen plates at tip of mouth have light tips, and mostly black
- 30 to 60 throat grooves
- Pectoral fins and tail are dark underneath

DISTRIBUTION

The sei whale is present in all of the world's oceans. This whale is rarely encountered within inshore areas of Newfoundland and Labrador, however, and most information about the animals in our waters comes from hunting records, aerial surveys and ship sightings.

Sei whales move northward along the continental slope in early summer. After spending their summers feeding in northern latitudes, seis return south in late fall. They breed and calve in southern latitudes during the winter. Exactly where their breeding and calving grounds are located is not known.

IDENTIFICATION

The sei whale is the third-longest baleen whale, after blue and fin whales. Colouration varies widely among sei whales, although the animals are generally bluish-grey, with lighter hues of grey along the sides. The skin of a sei whale is typically mottled with a large number of whitish scars.

Sei whales feeding.   Jon Lien

Seis can be easily confused with fin whales. Both species have similar body sizes, colouration and dorsal fins. However, a sei dorsal fin is tall and slender and located slightly further towards the head compared to those of fin and blue whales. The yellowish-white right lower jaw of the fin whale also distinguishes it from the sei.

Sei whales do not raise their flukes above the water when diving. Rather than arch their backs to dive, seis simply slide under the surface. Upon surfacing, the dorsal fin is visible at the same time as the whale blows. This is unlike fin whales, which blow shortly before the dorsal fin becomes visible.

BIOLOGY

The sei whale presents many challenges to scientists attempting to study this species. Their body size, colouration and dorsal fins are similar to fin whales, and they share the same general migration patterns.

Seis are also difficult to study because their behaviours are unpredictable. They may be regular visitors to a feeding area, but then disappear for a number of years. Because of this, and the expense associated with conducting surveys for marine mammals on the open ocean, there is a poor understanding of population size and distribution. Much of the information currently available has

Above/right: Sei whale   Doug Perrine / SeaPics.com

been derived from hunting records.

The diet of sei whales is thought to mainly consist of copepods and euphausiids (krill). One of their feeding methods involves skimming along the surface, a practice also used by right whales and bowheads. In fact, they often share the same feeding grounds as right whales. Seis also feed by engulfing small schooling fish. They are known to follow offshore plankton blooms, which often occur at the edge of continental shelves.

Sei whales reach a size of fifteen metres and a weight of nineteen tonnes. As with all the baleen whales, females are larger than males, and seis reach sexual maturity at eight to ten years. Calving intervals are two to three years, and females have a gestation period of about one year. Calves are weaned after six to nine months. The animals are known to live for about sixty years.

Seis are believed to be among the swiftist of all baleen whales, with one animal clocked at fifty-six kilometres per hour.

HUMAN INTERACTION

Commercial whalers turned their attention to sei whales after they had decimated other baleen whales, including the right, bowhead, blue, fin and humpback. Seis were prized for their meat, and they were the last large whale to be commercially hunted in Canadian waters. Records show 239 seis were landed in Newfoundland ports, and about 1,000 in Nova Scotia.

Little is known about their current population, with an estimate of less than 2,500 animals living in the western north Atlantic.

MINKE WHALE
(Balaenoptera acutorostrata)

IDENTIFICATION
- Smallest baleen whale (less than 10 metres)
- Blow difficult to see
- Tall, curved dorsal fin
- White band on pectoral fins
- Does not lift tail when diving
- Unpredictable surface movements
- Can be confused with small fin or sei whales

- Narrow, pointed head
- Short cream-coloured baleen, up to 30 cm long
- 50-70 throat grooves
- White belly
- Pectoral fins long, narrow and pointed

DISTRIBUTION

The minke is one of the most abundant of the world's whale species. It lives in both inshore and offshore areas, and in polar, temperate and tropical waters. Worldwide, there may be close to one million minkes, although it is now suspected that there is more than one species of minke whale. There are no reliable population estimates in eastern Canadian waters, but they are common throughout the summer, fall and early winter.

Minkes in Newfoundland and Labrador waters generally follow the same migration pattern as other baleen whales. They leave warm subtropic waters in early spring, and reach their New-foundland feeding grounds by April. Minkes travel north to Labrador, where large concentrations have been seen in recent years. Sightings throughout the year indicate that some animals are permanent residents.

Patrick Abgrall, DFO
A minke whale in the Laurentian Channel. Its blow is barely visible.

IDENTIFICATION

Minkes are commonly spotted in Newfoundland and Labrador waters and have a season coinciding with humpbacks. Both species are often seen feeding in close proximity. Minkes travel around coastal areas by themselves or with a calf.

Dive patterns of the minke are erratic and their surface regime is hard to predict. Often, you will hear a minke before you see it. The blow is usually only seen in good weather. Minke backs are black to greyish, with white or grey bands along the sides. The belly is bright white. Its dorsal fin is curved like a sickle and is seen as the animal emerges from the water. The head is small and pointed, with a single ridge running down the middle.

If you are close enough to an animal, you may see the white band on its flippers – this immediately identifies the whale as a minke. Southern hemisphere minkes do not have such a pronounced flipper band. The baleen of the minke is the smallest of the baleen whales (30 cm), and is creamy or yellowish in colour. Minkes do not lift their tails when diving. They are rarely seen breaching in our waters.

BIOLOGY

This whale is slightly larger than one of its only natural predators, the killer whale. Its diet includes capelin, cod and krill. The reproductive life of the minke resembles that of the other baleen whales. They become sexually mature at age seven. The gestation period lasts for

Photos by Patrick Abgrall

Above: Minke whale preparing to dive. Right: Minke whale in Bonne Bay.

eleven months and the mother provides milk for six months. Minkes reproduce more frequently than the other baleen whales and can have a calf every year. Their lifespan is about fifty years.

HUMAN INTERACTION

Historically, the minke was not hunted commercially because it is small, fast and produces little blubber. Minkes accounted for four per cent of the 20,000 whales that were killed in Newfoundland waters. However, it became the species of choice for modern-day whalers after the larger species had become commercially extinct. Minkes are now hunted in limited numbers for their meat by Japanese, Norwegian, Icelandic and aboriginal whalers.

Although not the prime target for whale watching, the minke provides a good backup if there are no humpbacks around. They have been observed picking up cod that falls from gillnets on the Virgin Rocks region of the Grand Banks. Fishermen on the southern Avalon Peninsula have had "pet" minkes around their cod traps. One whale, known by fishermen as Spot, would hover underneath fishing boats as they pulled in gill nets, and scavenge falling cod.

Minkes are the second-most common whales to become entrapped in fishing gear in our waters, after humpbacks. Unlike other whales that become entangled in netting or ropes, minkes are known to assist rescuers in their own release by opening their mouths and shaking the gear off.

HUMPBACK WHALE
(Megaptera novaeangliae)

IDENTIFICATION
- Large whale (12 to 14 metres)
- Raises tail when diving
- Long white pectoral fins
- Bushy blow
- Usually seen in groups
- Has a hump on dorsal fin
- Many "knobs" on head
- Barnacles on chin, tail and fins
- Throat grooves highly pro-nounced
- Black baleen, up to 90 cm long

DISTRIBUTION

Humpbacks are the most abundant of the large whales in Newfoundland and Labrador. They are commonly found throughout all coastal and offshore regions.

Humpbacks follow much the same migratory routes as other baleen whales that live in the northwest Atlantic. They travel to colder, northern regions for feeding and return to warmer, southern waters for breeding and calving. Four separate feeding stocks have been identified in North American waters: Newfoundland and Labrador, Gulf of St. Lawrence, Gulf of Maine, and western Greenland. There are approximately 11,000 humpbacks in the northwest Atlantic, with the Newfoundland feeding stock being the largest. Breeding and calving occur in the West Indies between December and April. Most humpbacks begin arriving in Newfoundland waters in April and range north to Labrador. Some whales remain late into the year and a resident group may overwinter here.

Claudio Corbelli, Whale Research Group

Humpback showing its dorsal fin, prior to diving near Witless Bay.

Wayne Ledwell

A humpback whale lying on its side, showing its tail and a pectoral fin, near Twillingate.

IDENTIFICATION

Its distinctive physical characteristics and unique behaviours make the humpback easy to identify. Other large whale species may raise their tails while diving, but they are rarely seen close to shore around Newfoundland and Labrador.

Humpbacks are so named because their dorsal fin sits on top of a hump. The fin is usually curved, but may be floppy, chewed and sometimes even missing entirely. There are knobby protrusions around the .head and jaws. One fisherman, upon seeing an entrapped humpback in his nets, said he did not know the species,

Claudio Corbelli, Whale Research Group
Three humpback whales traveling together at Witless Bay.

Deb Young, O'Brien's Whale and Bird Tours
The blow of a humpback whale near Bay Bulls is clearly visible. Note its pectoral fins, which are seen beneath the water.

but that its "knobs" made it look like an alligator.

The long white pectoral fins are a distinctive identifying feature of humpbacks. These flippers are one-third the length of the body and tapered like airplane wings. The leading edges are covered with barnacles and bumps.

The tail is broad, serrated and sometimes missing large chunks due to attacks by killer whales. Colouration on the underside of the tail can range from all black to all white, with variations in

Humpback whale lunge-feeding in Fortune Bay.   Wayne Ledwell

Claudio Corbelli, Whale Research Group
Humpback whale lunge-feeding near St. Anthony.

between. Humpbacks can be individually identified by their particular tail markings, which are easily photographed before the whale
dives.

The blow is usually "bushy," and can aid in distinguishing a
humpback from other large whales, such as fins and blues.

A humpback will often swing its large fins, slap its tail on the
surface, or even leap clear out of the water. These acrobatic qualities endear the humpback as a whale-watcher's delight.

Deb Young, O'Brien's Whale and Bird Tours
A humpback, near Bay Bulls, looking up.

BIOLOGY

Female humpbacks are about one metre longer than males, and become sexually mature at five years of age. Every two years a female may bear a calf, following a ten- to twelve-month gestation period. The calves are weaned after one year, although juveniles may stay with their mothers for up to two years.

Humpbacks eat a variety of schooling fish, but their food of choice while in Newfoundland and Labrador waters is capelin. This small fish forms dense spawning and schooling concentrations and is the main prey of numerous species of larger fish, seabirds and whales. They are "fast food" for humpbacks, who have developed specialized feeding techniques for capturing them. One common method is for a whale to barrel into a school of them with its mouth wide open. Another technique involves one or more animals releasing air under water while encircling a school of fish, thereby concentrating the fish within a "bubble net." This feeding method is unique to humpbacks. They have also been documented in Newfoundland waters "cliff feeding," whereby a whale uses a cliff as a barrier to trap fish. As it lunges at the fish, the momentum sometimes forces the whale partially out of the water and onto the rocks.

Humpbacks are one of the most studied of the great whales. The animals are frequently recorded singing at their southern breeding

Jon Lien

Humpback cow and calf.

Claudio Corbelli, Whale Research Group

Humpback breaching near St. Anthony, showing its long pectoral fin. Note the yellow barnacle patch under its head.

and calving grounds. These songs can last for half an hour and are repeated continuously. Among humpbacks, only the males sing, with the songs changing as the breeding season progresses.

Jon Lien

Above: A humpback being released from fishing gear. Right: Humpback tail. The scarring and pigmentation are used by scientists to identify and track individual animals. Photo by Claudio Corbelli, Whale Research Group

HUMAN INTERACTION

The qualities that make the humpback the favourite of whale watchers were the same ones that enabled commercial whale hunters to severely deplete stocks. Its major breeding and feeding regions are close to areas inhabited by people, and when feeding it tends to stay in one area for extended periods of time. During the whaling era 1,414 humpbacks were reported killed in Newfoundland and Labrador waters, accounting for about seven per cent of the whales taken here. The only hunting of humpbacks permitted today is in St. Vincents and the Grenadines in the Caribbean, where two animals per year are killed under aboriginal rights legislation. The humpback population in the northwest Atlantic is growing and no longer appears to be in imminent danger.

But some threats remain. Humpbacks and humans share many of the same places in search of fish. Unfortunately, the humpback is an accident waiting to happen when it comes to fishing gear. Many animals become entangled in fishing nets and ropes, due in part to their long, barnacle-ridden pectoral fins and tails, which can become snagged. More than 1,300 have been reported entangled in Newfoundland and Labrador waters since 1979.

NORTHERN RIGHT WHALE
(Eubalaena glacialis)

IDENTIFICATION
- Large whale (up to 17 metres)
- No dorsal fin
- Large rough white patches of callosities on head
- "V"-shaped blow
- Tail is all black with a deep notch
- Lifts tail vertically prior to diving
- Slow swimmers
- No throat grooves
- Dark baleen, two metres long
- Mouth is greatly arched
- Head is 1/4 the length of its body
- Pectoral fins are somewhat square and paddle-like
- Belly black with white patches

DISTRIBUTION

The northern right whale originally ranged throughout the temperate latitudes of the Atlantic and Pacific oceans. Intensive hunting greatly reduced populations, however, and now only small numbers exist in the north Atlantic Ocean. There are approximately 300 right whales living in the northwest Atlantic, ranging from Florida to Newfoundland.

During the winter, some right whales remain feeding in Cape Cod off Massachusetts, while others travel down the coast to calve off Florida and Georgia. The Roseway Basin in the Bay of Fundy off southern Nova Scotia is a major summer feeding area. Small numbers can be found elsewhere on the Scotian Shelf and as far west as the Gaspé Peninsula. Occasional sightings occur in other areas of the Gulf of St. Lawrence and around Newfoundland.

Patrick Abgrall

Two right whales in the Bay of Fundy. The "V"-shaped blow is used to distinguish right whales from other whale species.

Danielle Dion

Right whale tail.

Claudio Corbelli

The snout of a right whale in the Bay of Fundy is seen in both images. The callosities are a distinguishing feature of this species.

Claudio Corbelli

IDENTIFICATION

The northern right whale is stocky compared to more stream-lined species such as fin and blue whales. Their jaws are strongly bowed and the head has a distinctive arch. Right whales appear dark from the ocean surface, and their backs may be mottled. As with all whales, there is no difference in skin colouration between males and females. There are irregular white patches on the belly and throat.

The right whale has no dorsal fin. Their blow is "V" or heart-shaped, when seen from ahead of, or behind, the animals. Their large flukes, stretching six metres in length, are black and deeply

Right whale breaching.

Pat Abgrall

notched, with smooth trailing edges. Growths, or callosities, occur on the head, behind the blowhole, the corners of its chin, around the lower jaw, and above the eyes. The largest area of rough patches is located atop the head and is called the "bonnet." This area of hardened skin is home to large barnacles and thousands of whale lice, which give the growths a creamy or light yellow colour. The number, size, placement and shape of those callosities are a principle means of identifying individual right whales.

These animals can be seen alone or in small groups. They are often quite active at the surface, engaging in flipper-slapping, lobtailing, and breaching. It is considered an inquisitive whale, and may sometimes approach boats. Right whales can be confused with their Arctic cousin, the bowhead whale.

BIOLOGY

There are three populations of right whales throughout the world, which are now considered to be separate species: the north Atlantic (*Eubalaena glacialis*), the north Pacific (*E. japonica*), and the southern hemisphere (*E. australis*).

The right whale grows up to seventeen metres in length, with males being about one metre shorter than females. They produce a single calf after a pregnancy of one year. Calves, measuring four to five metres at birth, are born in the fall and winter months. A calf will nurse for about one year and spend another year with its mother. They become sexually mature at seven to ten years, with intervals between calving of three to four years. Right whales are thought to live for about seventy years.

Right whales migrate to Canadian waters to feed on zooplankton – the insects of the sea. Grazing right whales may be seen skim feeding at the surface, with their mouths open and baleen visible. Apart from being one of the stockiest whales, the right is also one of the hairiest. On close inspection, one can see individual hairs on the tips of the upper and lower jaws.

HUMAN INTERACTION

The right whale was dubbed the "right" whale to hunt, because the animals are slow swimmers and yielded large volumes of highly valuable blubber and baleen. The carcasses also floated after the animals had been killed, which made them easier to process than some other whale species.

By 1880, the right whale was almost wiped out. One of the first whales to be hunted in North America is now Canada's most endangered and the most intensively studied. Human activities still haunt the right whale. Deaths through ship collisions and entanglements in fishing gear limit the chances for recovery of this species. Measures undertaken to protect right whales include the shifting of international commercial shipping lanes in the Bay of Fundy in order to funnel ships around the main right whale feeding areas. Regulations to decrease entanglements in fishing gear are also being enforced in the United States. In both Canada and the United States, whale-watching vessels must maintain a distance of at least 500 metres from a right whale. Because of its rarity and active surface behaviour, the northern right whale is one of the most important target species for the whale-watching industry in the Bay of Fundy.

Right: A right whale lying on its side, showing a pectoral fin.

Photo by Pat Abgrall

BOWHEAD WHALE

(Balaena mysticetus)

IDENTIFICATION

- Up to 15 metres long
- No dorsal fin or dorsal ridge
- Large head, up to 1/3 of total length
- Strongly curved mouthline
- Smooth blue-black back
- Ridge between blowholes, with depression behind them
- Tall, "V"-shaped blow
- Creamy to bright white patch on chin, with irregular black spots
- Pectoral fins more pointed than a right whale, 1.8 metres long
- Deeply notched, wide tail
- Longest baleen of all whales, up to 4 metres long
- No throat grooves

DISTRIBUTION

Bowhead whales are a circumpolar species that lives along the edges of Arctic pack ice. There are two groups of bowheads in the eastern Canadian Arctic: one in the Hudson Bay-Foxe Basin, and the other in the Baffin Bay and the Davis Strait area. Population estimates for these whales has recently been upgraded threefold to 3,000 - 4,000 animals. Bowheads winter in small numbers in waters off the northern Labrador coast.

During summer, bowhead populations follow retreating pack ice west and north into the Arctic. During the winter, they migrate east and southeast into the Labrador Sea and the Davis Strait.

The only recorded strandings in Newfoundland and Labrador of bowheads occurred in 1998 at Rattling Brook, in Green Bay, and in 2005 at Witless Bay on the Avalon Peninsula.

European whaling fleets hunted Labrador and Davis Strait bowheads over a 300-year period. The population had become commer-

Marc Gadoury

A bowhead whale surfacing in the eastern Canadian Arctic. Its white chin can be seen underwater.

cially extinct by the mid-nineteenth century.

IDENTIFICATION

European whalers named this species the Greenland right whale, while American whalers called it the bowhead, because the lower jaw resembles an archer's bow.

Among the bowhead's distinctive features is a whitish chin patch that extends to the rostrum. Some specimens also have grey stripes at the end of their tailstock.

Like its smaller cousin, the northern right whale, bowheads have no dorsal fin, possibly because their habitat includes heavy pack ice. The wide separation of its two blowholes causes its spout to look bushy and gives it a distinctive "V"-shape. Unlike the right whale, a bowhead's skin does not have callosities. When the whale is at the surface, the depression behind the blowhole gives the appearance of two separate humps.

Bowhead flukes are wide, about 7.6 metres long, and deeply notched. Like humpback and sperm whales, bowheads raise their tails vertically into the air before diving. The broad, paddle-like flippers are almost two metres long. Bowhead baleen can reach four metres in length, the longest of any whale. Stranded bowheads can be difficult to distinguish from right whales. A key difference between the two species is the shape of the pectoral fins – those of the bowhead are more tapered and less square than a right whale's fins.

BIOLOGY

Bowheads feed within Arctic icefields, where the waters are rich in tiny marine animals called zooplankton. The bowhead is especially adapted to living in these polar gardens. Bowhead whales are skim feeders, principally foraging on copepods and euphausiids (krill). They are capable of navigating under thick ice between areas of open water over long distances, and are adept at determining whether ice is thin enough for them to break through and create breathing holes. They typically remain at the water surface and blow a dozen or more times, before submerging again for fifteen to twenty minutes.

Little is known about the life cycle of bowheads, because of their small population and the difficulties faced studying these animals in the harsh Arctic environment. Bowheads are thought to become sexually mature at twenty-five years of age. Females can become pregnant every three to seven years and the gestation period lasts for approximately twelve to fourteen months. Bowheads are thought to be among the longest-living animals on the planet, and may live 100 years or more.

HUMAN INTERACTION

Bowheads are slow swimmers, which made them easy targets for commercial whalers. Harpooned animals would also float rather than sink after death, thereby making it easier to haul carcasses alongside vessels or drag them to shore for processing. They were particularly valuable to the whaling industry, since a single bowhead would produce fifteen tonnes of oil.

In 1530, Basque whalers set up the first whaling station in North America at Red Bay, Labrador. From 1530 to 1600, they hunted bowhead whales in Labrador. Some of those whalers, as well as the bones of the whales they hunted, lie buried at Red Bay.

The next era of bowhead whaling began in 1719, with European commercial fleets hunting the eastern Arctic population. By 1915, some 29,000 bowheads had been killed. This hunting left the population commercially extinct.

Bowhead whales remain protected throughout their range, except for a small, strictly managed Inuit hunt in Alaska. In recent years, there have been efforts in Nunavut aimed at reopening the traditional hunt. One bowhead was landed in 2002.

Although the hunting of bowheads has been virtually eliminated, the species faces other threats. Bowheads live in a fragile environment, where highly productive feeding areas can be negatively affected by climate change and oil spills.

Bowhead whale at the surface. Its bow-shaped jaw gives the animal its name.
(John K.B. Ford /Ursus/ SeaPics.com)

SPERM WHALE
(Physeter macrocephalus)

IDENTIFICATION
- Males up to 17 metres long, females 5 metres shorter
- Blowhole on front left side of head
- Blow is tilted at 45° angle
- Lifts tail when diving
- Triangular flukes are deeply notched
- Tail is dark on both top and bottom
- Long, low dorsal fin, with series of bumps
- Square head
- Skin looks wrinkled
- Large squarish pectoral fins
- Only whale over 10 metres in length with teeth
- 18 to 25 large peg-like teeth, visible in lower jaw only

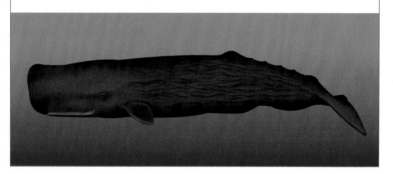

DISTRIBUTION
Sperm whales are an offshore, deep-water species and are found in all of the world's oceans. They venture north into Davis Strait and are sighted on the Grand Banks and around the Funk Island Bank off the northeast coast of Newfoundland during summer. Sperm whales are rarely seen in our shallow coastal waters. Those seen inshore are usually males.

During the spring and summer months, males migrate as far north as the high Arctic in the northern hemisphere, and to Antarctica in the southern hemisphere. As winter approaches, they join groups of females in temperate and tropical seas. Females stay in warm waters all year long.

The distribution of sperm whales in the north Atlantic is well documented due to records of the American sperm whale hunt, which started in 1712. There are no reliable population estimates

Dave Snow, Wildland Tours

A sperm whale diving in Trinity Bay.

for Newfoundland and Labrador, but worldwide numbers are thought to be approximately one million.

IDENTIFICATION

The sperm whale's scientific name, *Physeter macrocephalus*, is derived from Greek and means "long-headed blower." Unlike any other whale species, the single blowhole of the sperm whale is situated away from the centre of its snout – on the left-hand side – and the animals emit blows at a forty-five degree angle. This trait and the huge, square head are identifying features of this animal.

Sperm whales are dark grey or dark brown. The dorsal fin is long, low and thick, and a series of bumps protrudes from behind the dorsal fin towards the tail. Sperm whales usually lift their broad, triangular tails high when diving. They may dive for fifteen to twenty minutes, after which they rest at the surface for lengthy periods. Their skin is wrinkled and tough.

BIOLOGY

The sperm whale holds many records in the animal kingdom. It has the heaviest brain, the biggest nose and the largest teeth. Not only is it the largest toothed whale, but it hunts the mysterious giant squid. Sperm whales can dive to depths exceeding 3,000 metres.

Males are much larger than females: eighteen metres in length

Alison Loat

Sperm whale surfacing in Trinity Bay. This species has a dorsal ridge, rather than a dorsal fin.

compared to twelve metres for females. Males can weigh up to fifty tonnes. The diet and feeding habits of sperm whales are the subject of speculation and debate. Thousands of squid beaks have been found in the stomach of individual sperm whales, indicating that squid form an important part of their diet. Many animals bear sucker scars inflicted by the tentacles of giant squid. How they capture giant squid remains a mystery.

The lower jaw has large peg-like teeth, but it is not clear what purpose the teeth serve. They may be used for catching squid, but it is clear that they are able to feed without use of their teeth, because several otherwise healthy whales have been found with severely twisted and damaged lower jaws.

The white, luminous tinge of the lower jaw may be used to attract squid. It is also possible they use their jaw as a plow to sift the bottom for food. Pieces of fishing gear and other debris have been recovered from the stomachs of these animals, lending credence to this theory.

Sperm whales bear a single calf about every four years, and have a gestation period of sixteen months. Calves can nurse for long periods, often for more than four years. They live to be sixty to seventy years of age.

marinethemes.com/Tony Wu

Sperm whale diving.

HUMAN INTERACTION

The hunting of sperm whales has been the subject of fascination and legend for more than three centuries. Popularized by Herman Melville's book, *Moby Dick*, the sperm whale was intensively hunted for its blubber, spermaceti, ivory teeth and ambergris. The whale derives its common name from the spermaceti, a white wax-like substance found in its head which, when boiled down, produced high-quality oil. Early whalers thought this oil was the sperm of the whale. The gut of some sperm whales contains a brownish lumpy substance known as ambergris. It is thought that this material is deposited around squid beaks within the tissues of the gut. Large lumps can weigh more than 100 kilograms and had been extremely valuable to whalers. Ambergris was used as a fixative in the perfume industry and also as an aphrodisiac. It can occasionally be found floating in the ocean, presumably expelled by sperm whales.

Sperm whales were hunted along with other whales in Newfoundland and Labrador, with 425 landed at the various shore stations during the modern whaling era.

PYGMY SPERM WHALE
(Kogia breviceps)

IDENTIFICATION
- Small whale (2 - 3.5 metres)
- Dorsal fin is low and curved
- Steely grey colour
- Sometimes floats motionless at the surface
- Emits reddish-brown fluid when startled
- Shark-like appearance
- Blowhole slightly off-center

- Conical head, like a miniature sperm whale
- Tiny underslung lower jaw
- 10 - 16 curved, pointy teeth in each side of lower jaw (No teeth in upper jaw)
- Broad, short pectoral fins
- Tail broad, with slight notch

DISTRIBUTION

On Regatta Day, August 7, 2002, people living near the town of Little St. Lawrence on the Burin Peninsula were surprised by a strange little whale that repeatedly swam ashore, and eventually died. The whale had been swimming around the bowl-shaped harbour for a week. The animal turned out to be a pygmy sperm whale. This stranding, together with one on the French island of Miquelon off southern Newfoundland in 1989, was the most northerly sighting of this rare whale. Another four were reported stranded in other parts of Atlantic Canada during the twentieth century.

The pygmy sperm whale is so rarely observed that no estimates can be determined regarding population size. Distribution information is derived mainly from strandings in the Atlantic, Pacific and Indian oceans. Its known range in the northwest Atlantic lies

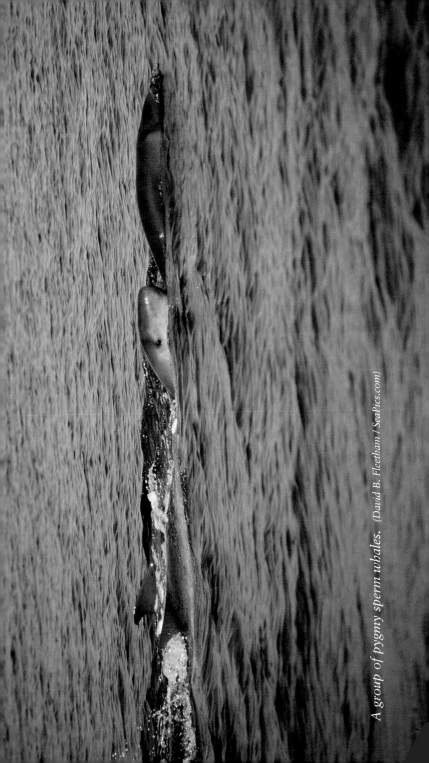

A group of pygmy sperm whales. (David B. Fleetham / SeaPics.com)

between the Gulf of Mexico and southern Newfoundland, with most sightings reported from the southern United States and the Bahamas.

IDENTIFICATION

The behaviour of this animal, when spotted at sea, is also mysterious. They are considered to be solitary, but have also been observed in groups of five or six. Pygmy sperm whales will lie motionless at the surface with the tops of their heads exposed. When startled by a boat, they sometimes emit a brown ink cloud before diving.

Their bodies are dark grey on top and a lighter grey underneath. The pygmy sperm whale bears some resemblance to the sperm whale, particularly the head, which is square at the back. However, unlike the sperm whale, the pygmy sperm whale has a pointed snout and a well-defined dorsal fin.

The blowhole of the pygmy sperm whale is at the top of its head, whereas the sperm whale has a large "S"-shaped blowhole located on the side of its head. The blow of pygmy sperm whales is bushy and low, and is not often observed. The dorsal fin is small, curved and located just beyond the mid-point of the back. The flippers are dark on top, chunky and tapered. The dark tail has a middle notch, but is not raised above the water while the whale is diving.

Stranded pygmy sperm whales are sometimes mistaken for sharks. The lower jaw is tiny and narrow, and the teeth curved, pointy and shark-like. There are a lightly coloured, crescent-shaped markings on the sides of its head that resemble gills. These are known as "false gills," which also gives the whale its shark-like appearance.

BIOLOGY

Not much is known about this little whale, and even the origin of the scientific name *Kogia* is a mystery. These whales, which are three to four metres long and weigh 400 kilograms, have been described as looking like sharks, porpoises, or sperm whales. The pygmy sperm whale has a small spermaceti organ in the back of its head.

Information about its eating habits has been obtained from examining the stomach contents of stranded individuals. It appears that pygmy sperm whales prey primarily on squid and fish, but some animals seem to have fed on prey species that live near the bottom. Squid beaks are not easily digested and numerous varieties of squid have been identified in the stomachs of pygmy sperm whales.

A peculiar feature of this species is a section of its lower intestine that is crammed with a thick chocolate-brown liquid that resembles oil. Since the whales appear to release a large dark cloud of this liquid just before fleeing, it has been suggested that this may serve as a decoy to distract predators. Pygmy sperm whales are preyed upon by large sharks, including the great white.

HUMAN INTERACTION

Due to its apparent rarity, no hunt was directed at the pygmy sperm whale, although there are records of whalers catching them. They occasionally become entangled in fishing gear, although this is not considered to be a survival risk to the species. There have also been reports of them swallowing floating plastics. The species is poorly researched, but it may be relatively common in some areas of the world.

In recent years, attempts have been made to rehabilitate stranded pygmy sperm whales by temporarily placing them in aquariums. Animals that survive are released back into the wild.

Julie Huntington

A dead pygmy sperm whale, stranded at Little St. Lawrence on the Burin Peninsula.

Julie Huntington

Pygmy sperm whales have long, sharp teeth.

KILLER WHALE
(Orcinus orca)

IDENTIFICATION
- Largest dolphin
- Males up to 9 - 10 metres females 5 - 6 metres
- Highly visible black & white colouration
- Tall triangular dorsal fin

- Rounded head with slight beak
- Large oval shaped pectoral fins
- Lives in stable family groups
- Large conical shaped teeth (10 to 12 on each side of both jaws)
- White patches around eyes
- Large dorsal and pectoral fins

DISTRIBUTION

Although killer whales are widely distributed throughout the oceans of the world, their abundance, distribution, migration and stock boundaries are poorly understood in the northwest Atlantic. Killer whales have been observed throughout the Newfoundland and Labrador region. Western north Atlantic populations appear to be restricted to northern latitudes.

Sightings are reported throughout our region, but killer whales are most often seen in the Strait of Belle Isle, off St. Anthony, in the fall, or near Battle Harbour in Labrador throughout the summer. They are also seen off Cape Spear, Witless Bay and the Bonavista Peninsula. They travel quickly, rarely staying in the same place longer than a few hours. They occasionally become stranded or entrapped in ice.

Dave Snow, Wildland Tours
Two killer whales swimming at the surface near Battle Harbour, Labrador.

IDENTIFICATION

Nature films, aquariums and the media have elevated the killer whale to a cult-like status. The animals are easily identified, due to their distinctive colouration and the tall dorsal fins of adult males. The head is black on top and white underneath. They have a white oval patch above and behind the eye and a grey to white "saddle" patch on the back behind the dorsal fin. Individuals can be identified by their eye patches, as well as by their "saddle" patches and dorsal fins. The killer whale is white underneath, but on the flanks the white sweeps up and onto its black sides. The most striking feature is the huge triangular-shaped dorsal fin of males. Females have smaller, curved dorsal fins. These whales are usually seen in small pods of two to six animals, traveling quickly through an area.

Killer whales are also known for their acrobatics, such as breaching (jumping out of the water), lob-tailing (striking their tails on the surface) and spy-hopping (raising their heads out of the water).

BIOLOGY

The killer whale is the largest member of the dolphin family and, with sharks, is among the top predators in the ocean.

They eat a variety of prey, including fish and squid, as well as other large whales, dolphins, seals and seabirds. Scars inflicted by killer whales upon other whale species, such as humpbacks, fins

Dave Snow, Wildland Tours
A male killer whale (foreground) is seen with a female and two calves.

and blues, are used by researchers to identify and track individual animals. Their large teeth make killer whales highly efficient predators. These whales, like all toothed whales, do not chew their food, but swallow it whole or in chunks. The large fins provide stability and quick movement, which is useful in pursuing prey.

Killer whales have some unique hunting habits. In the Antarctic, they have been observed bumping ice pans to tip seals into the water. They have also been seen chasing groups of narwhals ashore in Repulse Bay in the eastern Arctic, and even temporarily beaching themselves while capturing sea lions on shorelines in Argentina. In Norwegian waters, killer whales use the ocean bottom to corral and capture herring.

Most sightings of killer whales off Newfoundland and Labrador have occurred in areas where schools of fish, such as capelin and herring, are present. This suggests fish is the major component of their diet in our waters.

The maximum lifespan of killer whales is estimated to be fifty years for males and seventy to eighty years for females. However, their average life expectancy is thought to be about thirty years for males and fifty years for females.

Reproduction rates among all whale species may vary with the availability of prey. The calving interval of killer whales can be anywhere from two to twelve years. The gestation period is from one year to seventeen months.

Killer whales have a complex social structure based on groups of related females, called pods.

Claudio Corbelli

Male killer whale near St. Anthony. Note the tall dorsal fin of the male and the white "saddle" patch.

HUMAN INTERACTION

Killer whales were not targeted by commercial whalers. They were, however, fired upon to "keep the men active." They were regarded as a nuisance because the animals would sometimes compete with whalers for the whales they had killed. After a whale had been harpooned, killer whales would often appear and tear chunks from the carcass.

There are stories, however, of killer whales working in cooperation with Australian shore-based whalers in the late 1800s. The whales would alert hunters to the presence of humpbacks and, after a whale had been harpooned, the whalers would reward the killer whales by feeding them discarded carcasses (minus the blubber). There are isolated cases of captive killer whales attacking and, in at least two cases, killing people in aquariums. However, there are no documented cases of wild killer whales attacking humans. In some areas of the world, such as British Columbia, killer whales form the basis of a highly developed whale-watching industry.

Dave Snow, Wildland Tours

Male killer whale cruising close to shore in Labrador.

Dave Snow, Wildland Tours

The tail of a humpback whale, with bite marks inflicted by killer whales. These marks are used by whale researchers to identify and track individual animals.

A pod of killer whales near Battle Harbour, Labrador. (Tanya Bowen, DFO)

LONG-FINNED PILOT WHALE

(Globicephala melaena)

IDENTIFICATION

- Medium-sized (up to 6 metres)
- Usually seen chasing squid in large groups during late summer and early fall
- Rounded head gives it the name "pothead"
- Stocky build
- Long, thin, tapered, black flippers

- Dorsal fin is thick and set forward of mid-back
- Large bulbous head
- Short beak
- White "anchor" patch under chin
- One single grey belly stripe
- 8 to 12 pairs of peg-like teeth on each side of upper and lower jaws

DISTRIBUTION

The long-finned pilot whale, also known as the pothead, is a common species in Newfoundland and Labrador waters and is abundant worldwide. It is distributed in all cold and temperate waters, with the exception of the north Pacific. Pilot whales can be found pursuing squid inshore during the summer and autumn months. During the winter, they migrate out to the continental shelf of the Grand Banks and into the southern United States.

Pilot whales are generally an offshore species, but herds of the animals can be seen in the deeper bays of Newfoundland. Aerial survey work in the 1980s suggests about 14,000 pilot whales reside in Newfoundland and Labrador waters, but little is known of stock structure, migration and wintering habits off eastern Canada. It is generally assumed that they winter east of the Grand Banks,

Wayne Ledwell

Pilot whales in the Orphan Basin region of the Grand Banks.

although historically large herds of eighty or more have been hunted and seen inshore during the months of January and February.

IDENTIFICATION

Pilot whales are a medium-sized toothed whale, and are frequently found in inshore areas when squid are present. They are rarely seen alone, but travel in large groups of tens to hundreds of animals. They are relatively easy to identify at sea, due to the prominence of their wide, curved dorsal fin, which is set on a broad base, forward on the back. Females have a less prominent, but more pointed, dorsal fin than males.

They are known as "potheads" because the head bears some resemblance to a cooking pot. In older males the forehead is so large that it often overhangs the beak. Potheads have long, narrow pectoral fins that are so curved they have the appearance of an elbow. The fins are one-fifth the total length of the whale. The torso is torpedo-shaped and narrows at the tailstock. The tail flukes are small, pointed and have a slight middle notch.

Pilot whales are completely black, except for a white "anchor" patch under the chin and a narrow grey band running down the belly. Some whales also have a faint grey triangular "saddle" patch behind the dorsal fin.

The animals are often observed lying motionless at the surface, presumably resting. Individual pilot whales will often raise their heads above the water, a behaviour known as "spyhopping." When they do this, their white "anchor" patch can be observed.

BIOLOGY

The pilot whale is the third largest member of the dolphin family, after the killer whale and false killer whale. They are highly vocal and emit a wide range of whistles and clicks.

The diet and distribution of pilot whales is closely tied to squid abundance and migration. However, they also take other fish species such as cod and Greenland halibut (turbot). They coordinate their hunting activities by encircling schools of fish.

Pilot whales usually live about forty-five years, although animals as old as sixty have been reported. Females attain sexual maturity at age six and males at twelve. They weigh about 1.5 to three tonnes. The average length for males is five meters, with females being shorter. Pilot whales have a calf about every three years, following a gestation period of twelve months. Calves are born between June and November and nurse for almost two years.

Pilot whales are highly social, and entire herds are known to follow a leader ashore and beach themselves. Mass strandings of this species occur with some regularity in various parts of the world. Mass strandings have been recorded in Newfoundland, one of which occurred in 1979 at Point au Gaul on the tip of the Burin Peninsula when 139 pilot whales beached themselves. Point au Gaul, with its gently sloping headland that juts into the sea, is typical of the topography for mass strandings of pilot whales.

HUMAN INTERACTION

Scientists have derived valuable knowledge about the species from the Newfoundland pilot whale drive fisheries, where herds of animals were driven ashore and slaughtered. Between 1948 and 1971, approximately 54,000 pilot whales were taken during Newfoundland drive fisheries, mainly at Dildo and Chapel Arm. Drive fisheries for pilot whales are still conducted on the Faroe Islands.

In Newfoundland, pilot whales were mainly hunted to supply meat to the fox farming and pet food industries. Oil and fertilizers were also manufactured from pilot whales.

Currently, the species is not generally considered to be in immediate danger.

Pilot whales in the Orphan Basin. The head of a newborn calf is visible. (Wayne Ledwell)

NARWHAL
(Monodon monoceros)

IDENTIFICATION
- Small whale (up to 5 metres)
- Only whale with a tusk (males)
- Mottled, grey-brown whale
- Underside is lighter in colour
- Small round head

- No dorsal fin
- Short, turned-up pectoral fins
- Fan-shaped tail, with deep notch
- Frequently raises head out of water when swimming

DISTRIBUTION

Narwhals are found in the Arctic Ocean. In eastern Canada, there are two populations of narwhals – one in the Hudson Bay area with about 2,000 animals and a much larger stock of 20,000 in Baffin Bay and Lancaster Sound.

Narwhals move north as sea ice recedes in the spring, and migrate south as winter approaches. They usually travel in groups of four to twenty, but during migration often form larger herds, sometimes numbering in the thousands. Although usually not seen below the Arctic Circle, solitary narwhals occasionally wander into the bays and fiords of Labrador and Newfoundland. A narwhal spent the spring and summer of 2003 in Conception Bay, staying close to icebergs in the area.

IDENTIFICATION

The word narwhal is from an old-Norse term referring to a dead floating person. The scientific name of the species is *Monodon monoceros*. This is derived from the Greek *monos* (single) and *odontos* (tooth). This tusk, which is found only in males, is the most

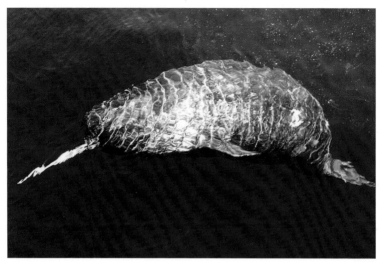

DFO

A male narwhal in Conception Bay.

obvious feature distinguishing narwhals from belugas, the only other whale that is likely to be confused with this species.

Newborn narwhals are a uniform dark grey, but as they mature the animals become mottled with dark spots. As adults, the animals become increasingly pale. The head is small and rounded, and the top jaw is slightly upturned.

Like the beluga, the narwhal has no dorsal fin, and both species have a similar body shape. Not only does the narwhal differ from other whales by having a long tooth, but the tail varies from all other species. Narwhal tails are convex on the trailing edge, which gives them a fan shape.

BIOLOGY

Male narwhals are somewhat larger than females and can reach four to five metres in length and weigh 1,600 kilograms. Narwhals have only two teeth, but in males one (and occasionally both) of these teeth becomes a tusk that grows from the left side of the upper jaw. This tusk, which is hollow and spiraled counterclockwise, can grow to two metres in length.

Narwhals are among the deepest-diving whales, often reaching depths of 1,000 metres or more. Their diet is varied and includes arctic cod, Greenland halibut (turbot), squid, shrimp and mollusks.

Narwhals are adept at surviving in ice-covered waters and can break through ice ranging from ten to fifteen centimetres thick with

Jon Lien

A group of male narwhals traveling in the Eastern Arctic.

their backs. They also use breathing holes made by seals, and take advantage of large rolling icebergs to keep waters open. Despite its ability as a navigator amidst pack ice, narwhals are sometimes trapped in small isolated areas of open water that have not yet frozen over. These entrapments provide a source of food for Inuit hunters and, occasionally, for polar bears. Large groups of more than 1,000 narwhals have been documented dying or being killed after being trapped in this manner. Killer whales are also a predator, driving groups of narwhals ashore or deeper into the pack ice.

Narwhals have a gestation period of close to fifteen months. Calves are born in summer and nurse for about two years. There is a three-year interval between calving. Narwhals can live for about fifty years.

HUMAN INTERACTION

The tusk of the narwhal has made it one of the best-known of all whale species. It was called the unicorn of the sea, and tusks collected by royalty were worth more than their weight in gold. Narwhal tusks even adorned the coronation throne of Denmark.

There is a limited hunt for narwhals in the eastern Canadian Arctic, including Baffin Bay. A more intensive hunt takes place along the west coast of Greenland. Narwhals are hunted for their tusks, as well as for their skins and meat. The skin and blubber, called maktaaq, is considered a delicacy among Inuit, and is rich in

DFO

Male narwhal at Spaniards Bay.

Vitamin C. There are concerns, however, that the Greenland hunt is unsustainable.

Narwhals may be adversely affected by noises from ships. They have been observed to change behaviour, stop moving about, or leave areas when large ships are present. Narwhals sometimes interact with human activities, however, and have been observed approaching boats and outboard motors.

Jack Lawson

Narwhals are sometimes attracted to boats.

BELUGA
(Delphinapterus leucus)

IDENTIFICATION
- Small whale (up to 5 metres)
- Young are grey, adults are white
- No dorsal fin
- Bulbous head
- Short beak, with flexible lips
- Distinct neck

- Only whale that can turn its head
- Up to 20 teeth on both the upper and lower jaws
- Middle notch in tail flukes
- Pectoral fins are short and broad

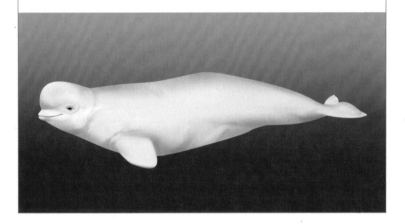

DISTRIBUTION
Belugas are primarily an Arctic whale, although an isolated population of approximately 600 animals lives in the Gulf of St. Lawrence.

The eastern Arctic population, which comprises 25,000 animals, lives in Baffin Bay, Davis Strait and the west coast of Greenland during the winter months. As summer approaches, they migrate north and west into the eastern Arctic.

Belugas can be seen off northern Labrador and solitary animals will occasionally visit the bays of Newfoundland. These are mostly juvenile whales.

They live in small groups for much of the year, but often form large migrating herds of up to 1,000 animals. As ice breaks up in the spring, belugas move into shallow waters of bays and estuaries.

Patrice Corbeil

A group of beluga whales in the Gulf of St. Lawrence.

IDENTIFICATION

The beluga is one of the few small whale species of the high Arctic. Adults are easily identified by their all-white colour. Their heads are small and rounded, with a prominent forehead, and their beaks are often described as appearing "smile-like." Belugas have no dorsal fin, a characteristic of whales that live amidst pack ice. Instead, belugas have a dorsal ridge, which is a series of raised bumps running down their backs. The flippers are short and broad. There is a distinct notch in the tail. Belugas are born light to dark grey, and become white – often with a yellowish tinge – by nine years of age. This whale is sometimes confused with the narwhal. They can also be difficult to spot among ice or waves.

BIOLOGY

The beluga, or "sea canary" as whalers called them, is among the most vocal of all whales and uses a variety of whistles, squeals, chirps and groans. Unlike other whales, belugas are able to turn their heads because their neck vertebrae are not fused. They are capable of deep dives, ranging to 350 metres or more, apparently feeding on both bottom-dwelling and free-swimming prey.

Belugas feed on a large variety of invertebrates and crustaceans. They also eat numerous species of fish, including squid, capelin, cod and Greenland halibut (turbot).

Unfortunately, many of the prey species of the beluga in the Gulf of St. Lawrence, such as American plaice, are heavily contaminated with toxic materials, including PCBs, insecticides and heavy metals. These pollutants accumulate in the tissues of belugas, which may eventually lead to death.

Male belugas range between three and five metres in length. Females are a little smaller. Both reach sexual maturity between four and seven years of age. Their average weight is 600 kilograms. Females bear a calf at approximately three-year intervals, with a gestation period of twelve to fourteen months. Calves nurse for a year and a half. Belugas have a lifespan of about thirty years. Their main natural predators are killer whales and polar bears.

HUMAN INTERACTION

Large-scale hunting of belugas in the eastern Arctic began during the mid-nineteenth century. The animals were sought for their blubber, which was used to manufacture soaps and lubricants. The animals were easy to find and kill, because they could be herded into shallow waters.

By the time commercial hunting ended, the St. Lawrence stock had been severely depleted, to fewer than 1,000 animals. The Inuit of the eastern Arctic still hunt limited numbers of belugas for subsistence purposes.

The St. Lawrence population is one of the most studied groups of whales, and research has shown high incidences of cancers and tumours from dozens of man-made toxic chemicals entering the estuary. Beluga carcasses may have such high concentrations of pollutants in their bodies that they have to be treated as toxic waste for disposal purposes.

Other dangers facing the beluga include degradation of their habitat through damming of rivers, dredging, and high-intensity noises associated with oil and gas exploration. Finally, there have been occasions where solitary juvenile belugas have sought out human activities at various locations in Atlantic Canada. They are attracted to propellers of outboard motors, a practice that often leads to an animal's demise.

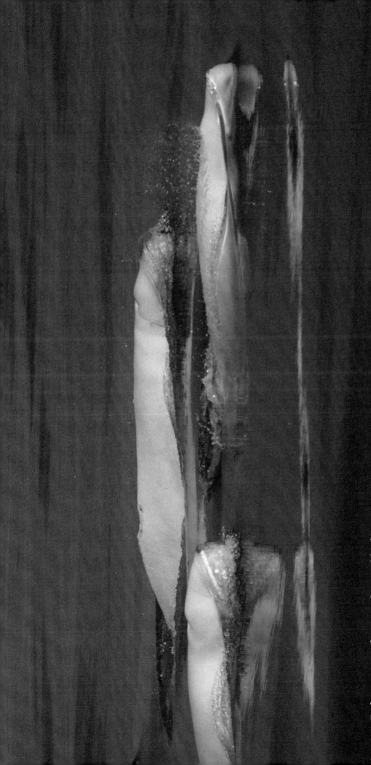

Belugas traveling in the Gulf of St. Lawrence. (Patrice Corbeil)

NORTHERN BOTTLENOSE WHALE
(Hyperoodon ampullatus)

IDENTIFICATION
- Medium-sized (7 - 9 metres)
- Round brownish body
- Prominent bulbous head (whitish in older males)
- Long "bottle-like" beak
- Can be seen in groups of 5 to 15

- Will often approach boats
- Does not raise tail when diving
- Two throat grooves under chin
- No tail notch
- Males may have two teeth visible at tip of lower jaw

DISTRIBUTION

The northern bottlenose whale is a deep-water species. It is typically found in areas of submarine canyons, seamounts, and other areas inside and outside continental shelves, at depths exceeding 1,000 metres. In the western north Atlantic they have been reported from New York state to Greenland. They also range as far east as the Barents Sea in northern Europe. Off eastern Canada, northern bottlenose whales are found in the Gully, an area north of Sable Island, Nova Scotia. A population of the animals lives in the Flemish Cap area of the Grand Banks, while a much larger group resides in the Davis Strait. The degree of interaction, if any, between these groups is unknown. Occasionally, an individual northern bottlenose whale will wander into inshore waters of Newfoundland, and other sightings have occurred off Labrador. Two stranded whales, a male and female, were found in Bonavista Bay in 2004.

DFO

Above/Below: Northern bottlenose whale in the Laurentian Basin.

DFO

IDENTIFICATION

The northern bottlenose whale is a member of a group of poorly understood medium-sized beaked whales. These whales are rarely observed because they live predominantly in remote regions of the ocean. Distinguishing between species of beaked whales at sea is difficult because they look similar from the surface. They can be identified through size differences, colouration, the shape of their foreheads and the lengths of their beaks. The northern bottlenose whale has a beak "like a bottle," hence the Latin *ampulla*, meaning flask.

This is a medium-sized whale, typically seven metres long. The northern bottlenose whale is brown to dark grey, and has a large bulbous forehead. Males are more easily identified than females because their forehead, known as a melon, whitens with age. Males usually have two cone-shaped teeth, which are visible at the tip of the lower jaw. Females have no teeth.

The dorsal fin of the northern bottlenose whale is sickle-shaped, and located about two-thirds of the way back from its snout. The flippers are small and tapered. The tail is broad and has no central notch. It has two throat grooves that widen into a "V" towards the back of the lower jaw. Northern bottlenose whales are often seen in groups of five to fifteen, and are known for their deep-diving ability. They have been recorded at depths of more than 1,000 metres, with dive times lasting up to an hour and a half. After diving, they remain resting at the surface for ten minutes or so. The blow is "bushy" and may be visible under good weather conditions. Northern bottlenose whales are known for their curiosity, and may approach boats and other man-made objects.

BIOLOGY

Because the northern bottlenose whale lives in some of the most inaccessible places on Earth, most information on its biology comes from stranded individuals and data collected during the days of commercial hunting. However, there is a small group of bottlenose whales living in and around the Gully that has been extensively studied. This population is estimated at 130 to 250 animals.

Their diet consists of squid and a variety of fishes, including Greenland halibut (turbot), skate, redfish and herring. Northern bottlenose whales are obviously able to catch prey despite their lack of teeth. It has been suggested they employ "suction feeding" as one method of capturing prey, but this has yet to be substantiated.

HUMAN INTERACTION

European whalers hunted the northern bottlenose whale extensively in the late nineteenth and early twentieth centuries. Between 1969 and the end of commercial whaling in Newfoundland in 1972, Norway took 824 bottlenose whales in the Labrador Sea. The whale was primarily hunted as a source of animal food and valuable spermaceti oil, which is found in its large bulbous head. Up to ninety kilograms of oil could be obtained from one whale. Groups of northern bottlenose whales will approach vessels, and since they will not leave injured companions, the animals became easy targets for whalers.

Since 2000, fishermen in the Davis Strait area have reported northern bottlenose whales interfering with longline fishing operations by stealing turbot from hooks. They are attracted to the sounds of ships, which they have learned to associate with food in the form of discarded fish. It is unknown what the extent of this problem really is. Some whales may become entangled in longline

DFO
Three northern bottlenose whales in the Gully, near Sable Island.

fishing gear.

Threats to the population include disturbances from seismic exploration surveys for oil and gas. They are also injured by ship strikes and entanglements in fishing gear. It was largely because of these threats to northern bottlenose whales in the Gully that the region was officially designated as a marine protected area in 2004.

Northern bottlenose whale lobtailing off Baffin Island.

SOWERBY'S BEAKED WHALE

(Mesoplodon bidens)

IDENTIFICATION
- Medium-sized (up to 5 metres)
- Small dorsal fin set midway on back
- Two teeth in lower jaw, visible in males only
- Generally found offshore; thought to inhabit underwater canyons and escarpments
- Slate-grey colour, lighter below
- Long thin beak
- Two throat grooves
- Scars common among males
- Small pectoral fins, dark on both sides
- Tail has no middle notch and dark on both sides

DISTRIBUTION

The Sowerby's beaked whale is also known as the North Sea beaked whale, because that was where the first specimen was discovered in 1800. Little is known of its distribution, but stranding information suggests a range covering most of the offshore waters of the north Atlantic. Sightings and strandings of these whales are rare, with most strandings in North America reported from the east coast of Newfoundland. Sightings at sea have occurred in Newfoundland waters. Sowerby's beaked whales have also been reported in the Gully, off Sable Island, Nova Scotia, either as individuals or in groups of up to six animals.

Sowerby's beaked whale (marinethemes.com/João Quaresma)

Wayne Ledwell

The tail of a Sowerby's beaked whale, which stranded at Conception Bay.

IDENTIFICATION

The Sowerby's has one of the most northerly distributions of any beaked whale species in the north Atlantic.

Many beaked whales look similar at sea unless you are able to approach an animal. They all have long, tapered bodies, small dorsal and pectoral fins, and similar foreheads, beaks and colouration. All are probably deep divers, sharing similar habitat around deep-water canyons at the edges of continental shelves. Very little is known about any of the beaked whales, except for the pilot whale. The Sowerby's differs mainly in the position of two teeth in the lower jaw of the males. Females and juveniles are likely impossible to identify at sea.

Sightings of Sowerby's beaked whales at sea are rare. When they have been seen, the long thin beak is visible above water as the animal surfaces. The rounded head tapers down to its beak, like that of a dolphin. Mature males usually have two teeth present in the middle of the lower jaw and these are visible when the animal has its mouth closed. Its long sleek body has a brownish to dark grey hue, with a lighter shade of grey underneath. The small, curved dorsal fin is situated just past the mid-point on its back. The side fins are dark on both sides, as is the tail. There is a middle notch in the tail flukes. Sowerby's beaked whales are generally unobtrusive at sea, and wary of boats. Their blow is not usually visible.

BIOLOGY

The Sowerby's beaked whale is one of six beaked whale species in the north Atlantic. It was first identified from a stranded specimen found in 1800 in Scotland, and named after James Sowerby, who first described it. Because of its apparent rarity, this whale's population structure, migration, distribution patterns and life history are poorly understood. Much of the known information comes from strandings along the coasts of the British Isles and Newfoundland, where mass strandings occurred involving six animals in 1986 and three more in 1987. Most of the fourteen stranded Sowerby's reported in Newfoundland have been on the northeast coast of the island, in the New World Island area. Sightings in other parts of the world have generally been in waters with depths ranging from 200 - 1,500 metres.

Wayne Ledwell

Whale researcher, Jon Lien, examining a dead Sowerby's beaked whale at New World Island in 2003.

Like other deep-diving whales, their food of choice appears to be squid. Squid beaks are not easily digested and thus leave a record in the stomach – which has been examined in stranded individuals – of what the animal has eaten. There is no information about migration or reproduction.

HUMAN INTERACTION

Due to their apparent rarity and secretive habits, Sowerby's were never hunted commercially, although some animals were occasionally taken. Recently, concerns have been raised about the apparent vulnerability of beaked whales to certain man-made, high-energy underwater sounds.

WHITE-BEAKED DOLPHIN
(Lagenorhynchus albirostris)

IDENTIFICATION
- Large dolphin (up to 3 metres)
- Short white beak
- Tall, curved, black dorsal fin
- Light grey colour on the back, behind dorsal fin
- An acrobatic species
- 44 to 56 teeth in both upper and lower jaws
- Teeth are fewer in number and larger than white-sided dolphins
- Underside is white
- Pectoral fins and tail are dark
- Sometimes attracted to boats

DISTRIBUTION

White-beaked dolphins occur only in the north Atlantic Ocean and are a common species throughout Newfoundland and Labrador waters. In the northwest Atlantic, they range from Cape Cod in the United States to Davis Strait and Greenland.

Although more abundant in inshore areas between June and October, they are also resident in our waters during the winter and spring. It is estimated that 4,500 white-beaked dolphins live off the coasts of Newfoundland and Labrador.

The animals can be seen throughout the region. Some of the best inshore viewing areas include the Strait of Belle Isle, southern Labrador, around St. Anthony and New World Island during the summer and fall. At times, small groups of the animals will repeatedly breach in perfect unison.

Jon Lien

Three white beaked dolphins, trapped by pack ice on the northeast coast of Newfoundland.

IDENTIFICATION

White-beaked dolphins can be mistaken for Atlantic white-sided dolphins, which share the same range. But the white-beaked is a more coastal and northerly species and is the dolphin most often seen off Newfoundland and Labrador.

Both species perform acrobatics and are fast swimmers. In addition, they share similar group structures, and generally travel in units of fifty or fewer animals. However, both dolphin species will sometimes form groups of over 1,000 individuals.

The white-beaked dolphin derives its name from its short, white beak. The dorsal fin is large, black and prominently curved. Behind this fin the white-beaked dolphin has a grey patch. It also has white and grey patches on its sides and flanks. These patterns distinguish it from its close relative, the Atlantic white-sided dolphin, which has a yellowish patch on its tailstock.

Pat Abgrall

White-beaked dolphin in the Gully, near Sable Island.

BIOLOGY

Little is known about the life cycle of the white-beaked dolphin, because the animals were not the focus of large-scale hunting and they do not do survive well in captivity. Much of what is known about this species comes from sightings at sea, strandings and ice-entrapments. Large groups of several hundred have been reported trapped in shifting pack ice close to shore around Newfoundland. However, unlike the white-sided dolphin, which is known to strand on beaches in large groups, white-beaked dolphins are more likely to strand as individuals.

White-beaked dolphins eat a variety of groundfish, including cod and haddock. They also pursue squid and pelagic schooling fish such as capelin, herring and mackerel.

They are sometimes seen foraging alongside large whales, such as humpbacks and fin whales, and occasionally with other dolphin species.

Only a limited amount of information is available regarding the reproductive cycle of the white-beaked dolphin. Pregnancies last about one year, and most calves appear to be born between May and September. Its lifespan is currently unknown. It is assumed that killer whales and large sharks are its natural predators.

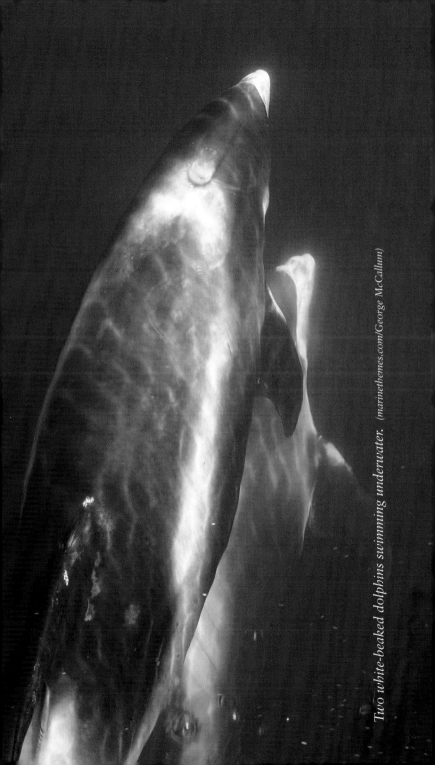

Two white-beaked dolphins swimming underwater. (marinethemes.com/George McCallum)

Hollis Yetman
A white-beaked dolphin, released after being stranded near Flat Bay.

HUMAN INTERACTION

White-beaked dolphins are sometimes entrapped in gillnets, although not in large numbers around Newfoundland and Labrador. Because they are often found with other whales, they were incidentally rounded-up in drive hunts for pilot whales in Newfoundland and elsewhere.

White-beaked dolphins appear to be curious about human activities at sea, and often can be seen riding the bow waves of boats and ships.

White-beaked dolphin, Witless Bay.
(Deb Young, O'Brien's Whale & Bird Tours)

ATLANTIC WHITE-SIDED DOLPHIN
(Lagenorhynchus acutus)

IDENTIFICATION

- Medium-sized dolphin (up to 2.5 metres)
- Short beak
- Upper jaw is black, lower jaw white
- Tall black dorsal fin
- White patches below dorsal fin
- Mustard-coloured patch on sides behind dorsal fin
- An acrobatic species
- Often seen with other whale and dolphin species
- 60 to 80 pointed teeth in both upper and lower jaws
- Pectoral fins are sickle-shaped, pointed, and dark in colour
- Thick, muscular tailstock
- Sometimes attracted to boats

DISTRIBUTION

The Atlantic white-sided dolphin has a wide range throughout the northwest Atlantic Ocean. Surveys from Nova Scotia to Virginia show 30,000 animals in that area, but its total population is unknown. There are no population estimates for Newfoundland and Labrador.

This is primarily a dolphin of the continental shelf, although it does travel inshore. They are often seen in groups of fifty to sixty in Newfoundland and Labrador waters. Larger groups of more than 1,000 animals have also been observed offshore.

Robin W. Baird / SeaPics.com

An Atlantic white-sided dolphin, with a common dolphin behind.

IDENTIFICATION

This dolphin has an elongated white patch along each side, with a distinctive mustard-coloured patch near the tail. Like most whales and dolphins, this species has a dark back. The belly is white with a grey stripe.

The upper jaw is black and the lower jaw white. The beak is less pronounced than that of the common dolphin. The tall, black dorsal fin is set at the midpoint of the back. This dolphin, like common and white-beaked dolphins, is an acrobatic animal, and is often seen breaching and lobtailing. It has short dive times of about one minute. It sometimes rides the bow wash of boats, although not as frequently as the white-beaked dolphin.

BIOLOGY

White-sided dolphins grow to a length of about two-and-a-half metres and can be easily mistaken for white-beaked dolphins. Their colouration is distinctive at close range, however, particularly if the yellowish patch on the flanks can be seen. Common dolphins have a similar patch, but this is located towards the head of the animal, before the dorsal fin.

The diet of the white-sided dolphin consists of squid, herring, mackerel and other schooling fish. They frequently accompany fin, humpback and long-finned pilot whales, as well as white-beaked dolphins. This is probably a food-related relationship, as all share similar prey.

White-sided dolphins have a calf every two to three years. Pregnancies last for almost one year and a calf is born during the summer. Newborns are about one metre in length, and calves nurse for eighteen months. White-sided dolphins have a lifespan of approximately twenty-five years.

More information has been accumulated about the biology of white-sided dolphins than about other species of dolphin because of their tendency to strand in large groups. Mass strandings and ice entrapments of white-sided dolphins have occurred along the coasts of Newfoundland and Labrador.

HUMAN INTERACTION

Because white-sided dolphins often feed in close proximity to other whale species, this made them vulnerable to commercial whalers, who caught them as incidental by-catches during drive hunts for pilot whales in Newfoundland and Labrador. There are reports of this species becoming entangled in fishing gear offshore in the Newfoundland region, but the effect of this mortality on the population is unknown. However, the species is not currently considered to be at risk.

COMMON DOLPHIN
(Delphinus delphis)

IDENTIFICATION
- Medium-sized dolphin (up to 2.4 metres)
- V-shaped "saddle" of colour on each side of dorsal fin
- Tan or yellow colouring on sides
- Black belly stripe
- Long, pointed beak
- Black eye patches
- An acrobatic dolphin
- Usually travels in groups
- 80 to 110 small pointed teeth in both upper and lower jaws
- Pectoral fins black and tapered
- Tail concave with a deep notch
- Will approach ships and bow-ride

DISTRIBUTION

The common dolphin is widely distributed in temperate, subtropical and tropical waters in all of the world's oceans. This dolphin is primarily an offshore species, but is occasionally seen in inshore areas of Newfoundland and Labrador.

During the summer, the common dolphin ranges from the southern Grand Banks to Georges Bank. They are usually seen in groups of thirty to 200 animals, but on the continental shelf they congregate into groups in excess of 1,000. Population estimates for the northwest Atlantic are in the range of 27,000.

IDENTIFICATION

Unlike the other two resident dolphin species of Newfoundland and Labrador, common dolphins are primarily offshore animals.

It is difficult to distinguish dolphin species from a distance, but

Pat Abgrall, DFO

Common dolphin breaching in the Laurentian Basin off Nova Scotia. Note the "saddle" patch beneath its dorsal fin.

at close range the common dolphin can be identified by its colouration. A swath of black, which runs from head to tail, dips into the light underside below the dorsal fin. This forms a "V" pattern.

Forward of the dorsal fin, the sides feature a swath of yellow or tan colouration. Behind the dorsal fin, a grey wave of colour sweeps to the tail.

The common dolphin has a long narrow beak. It has a black patch around the eyes, which continues to the beak. The flippers are black, although the upper sides are often tinged with grey. Its black dorsal fin is approximately forty cm in height and triangular.

There is nothing common about the behaviour of this multi-coloured dolphin. The animals frequently breach, and often ride the waves made by boats – and even the wash of large whales. Common dolphins are extremely active and fast. They also perform somersaults, and often slap their tails and chins on the water surface.

Pat Abgrall, DFO photos

Above/right: Common dolphin.

BIOLOGY

The common dolphin is highly vocal and emits a variety of whistles and clicks that sometimes can be heard above the water. It is a social species, usually seen in herds of thirty or more, and often in the company of white-sided dolphins and other large whales.

This dolphin feeds on short-finned squid, as well as schooling fish, such as capelin, herring and mackerel.

Common dolphins are approximately two metres in length and weigh 100 kilograms. They reach sexual maturity at about six years of age and mate during the spring and autumn. Females bear a calf every year or two, and have a gestation period of one year. Newborns are eighty centimetres long and nurse for six months.

HUMAN INTERACTION

Common dolphins sometimes travel into the bays of Newfoundland and Labrador, and individuals have occasionally stranded here. Because it is primarily an offshore species, it is incidentally trapped in gillnets on the southern Grand Banks. There has never been a commercial hunt directed at common dolphins.

HARBOUR PORPOISE
(Phocoena phoceana)

IDENTIFICATION
- Small whale (up to 1.7 metres)
- Round head
- No beak
- Travels singly or in groups of up to five
- Triangular dorsal fin
- Avoids boats
- Does not breach
- "Rolling" motion while swimming at surface
- 20 to 29 small spade-shaped teeth in both the upper and lower jaws
- Slight fluke notch

DISTRIBUTION

The harbour porpoise is one of the smallest of the world's whale species and lives throughout the north Atlantic and the north Pacific oceans. Off the east coast of North America, the harbour porpoise can be found from North Carolina to Baffin Island. There are thought to be three distinct populations in eastern Canadian waters: Newfoundland and Labrador, Gulf of St. Lawrence, and Bay of Fundy/Gulf of Maine.

Harbour porpoises are widely distributed around the island of Newfoundland and southern Labrador, and throughout the Gulf of St. Lawrence. They visit bays and harbours and migrate south in advance of the winter freeze-up and pack ice. Winter distribution is poorly understood, as are population estimates for the animals in Newfoundland and Labrador waters. There are an estimated 50,000 harbour porpoises in the Bay of Fundy/Gulf of Maine region. There is evidence that some porpoises from this area migrate down to the mid-Atlantic region of the United States in winter.

A harbour porpoise. The animal is known as the "puffin pig" among Newfoundland fishermen because of the sounds they emit when blowing at the surface. (Florian Graner / SeaPics.com)

Danielle Dion

The dorsal fin and tail of a harbour porpoise, while diving.

IDENTIFICATION

Like many whales, harbour porpoise backs are black and their sides are greyish and fade to white underneath. The head is rounded and, unlike dolphins, they do not have a beak. The teeth are small and wedge-shaped.

Due to their small size and shy nature, harbour porpoises are difficult to spot or follow on the ocean. The animals tend to stay away from moving ships and the sounds of outboard motors, and quickly disappear from sight when approached. A viewer may get only a glimpse of a harbour porpoise's dorsal fin, which is small, triangular and set behind the midpoint of the animal's back. As the porpoise comes up to breathe, its dorsal fin typically shows in a rolling motion. You will need a calm day to spot them, but they are easy to identify because of their small size and behaviour. They bob around, flicking their tails out like a young foal kicking its legs. Harbour porpoises emit a series of quick blows and then dive for five minutes or so, depending on the water depth. If you hear a porpoise blow, you may understand why fishermen call them "puffin pigs," as their breathing sounds like grunts.

Harbour porpoises are usually seen individually or in small groups. Based on reports of accidental catches in fishing gear, researchers know they are most often in Newfoundland and Labrador waters during the spring, summer and fall.

BIOLOGY

Information on the biology and reproductive cycle of harbour porpoises comes largely from entrapments in fishing gear. Strandings are rare and of single animals, and those that strand have usually been injured following collisions with fishing nets or ropes.

Harbour porpoises, like other toothed whales, eat squid, crustaceans and most fish species. They feed alone, unlike dolphins which are usually seen in large groups.

Harbour porpoises are preyed upon by killer whales and by great white sharks, whose range includes the Gulf of St. Lawrence and possibly the south coast of Newfoundland.

Harbour porpoises grow to a length of approximately 1.7 metres and weigh up to seventy kilograms, with females being larger than males. They become sexually mature at three to five years. Females have a gestation period of almost one year and calves nurse for eight months. A newborn calf is less than a metre long and weighs six kilograms. Harbour porpoises usually live for about fifteen years, but ages of up to twenty-three years have been recorded.

HUMAN INTERACTION

Whales and fishermen share the same waters, and fish for similar species at the same time, usually in summer and fall. The consequence of this is the accidental entrapment of marine mammals. Harbour porpoises are no exception. Each year, many porpoises become entangled and drown in various types of fishing gear in the waters of Newfoundland and Labrador. It is unknown what long-term effect these deaths may have on the overall population.

There appear to be areas where harbour porpoises become entangled more frequently than others. These regions include St. Mary's Bay, the Burin Peninsula, the southwest coast and around Fogo Island.

Harbour porpoises that live in the mouth of the St. Lawrence River during the summer are affected by the runoff of industrial and agricultural chemicals, including PCBs and pesticides. These compounds are known to affect the reproduction and health of other marine mammals, such as belugas, but the specific effects on harbour porpoises are unknown.

Because of their aversion to boats and noises, and the high levels of acoustics used in undersea exploration, harbour porpoises may be forced away from important habitat areas. Native people occasionally hunt these animals in the northern part of their range.

ACKNOWLEDGEMENTS

This book would not be possible without the help of many individuals. Foremost to thank is Jon Lien, for teaching me about whales and how to work through the serious and recurring problem of whales and their entanglement in fishing gear. He also made possible many of the images in this book through the Whale Research Group, Memorial University.

Scientists who study whales often spend their lives putting together small pieces of the puzzle about where whales live, where they are born, what they eat and how they interact. The information on life histories of whales presented in this book is possible because of the work by scientists in Newfoundland and Labrador and elsewhere.

Finding images for this book proved challenging and we tried our best to include local pictures. Thanks to Patrick Abgrall, Claudio Corbelli, Dave Snow of Wildland Tours, Deb Young, O'Brien's Whale and Bird Tours, and Jack Lawson of the Department of Fisheries and Oceans. Thanks also to Hollis Yetman, Marc Gadoury, Tanya Bowen, Danielle Dion, and to others who presented us with images.

Among those who read the text and made valuable suggestions were my spouse Julie Huntington, Steven Benjamins, Brian Jones, Claudio Corbelli and Krista Koch. Others who were dedicated to completing this book include Elaine Frampton, who completed the whale artwork, designer John Andrews, and publisher Gavin Will.

To the fishing people, community members and fisheries and conservation officers of Newfoundland and Labrador who assist with whale disentanglements and strandings, this book is really for you. Long may your big jib draw!

Wayne Ledwell

In memory of my mother, Marion Ledwell.

Christina Folger

Author Wayne Ledwell at Great Island near Tors Cove, disentangling a whale from a cod trap.

WAYNE LEDWELL is a former fish harvester from Calvert, a community on the southern shore of the Avalon Peninsula in Newfoundland.

Wayne earned a Masters Degree in Marine Management from Dalhousie University. He has been involved in releasing whales and other marine animals from fishing gear since 1988. He and Julie Huntington operate the Whale Release and Strandings Group in Newfoundland and Labrador.

Wayne lives in Portugal Cove - St. Philip's with his three children: Noah, Sebastian and Abigail.